ALICE
IN
CORNFIELDS

Memories of an Iowa Farm Girl

By Alice Hammond Brook

THE HOUSE ON THE HILL

There were five of us Hammond Girls and we lived in a farmhouse at the top of a hill in Iowa. Dad was a tall, blue-eyed cowboy from Wyoming, but my Mom grew up on a farm just across the river. My big sisters, Hope, Chloe, Audrey, and Janice, were all born in Wyoming. Their mother, Carrie, died when they were very young, and Dad brought his little girls to Iowa to live near their mom's family. After he got started farming, he met my mother, and they got married and had me. We had lots and lots of aunts and uncles and cousins; so many that it was hard to remember who was related to whom, but it didn't really matter. I always knew I was really lucky to have a three-sided family, even though it wasn't always comfortable to have so many relatives watching us, feeling free to give us advice, and making sure our parents were aware of all of our misdeeds.

I was so very fortunate to be born into the Hammond/Duffy family, growing up during the post-war economic boom in Iowa. WWII was over; Uncle Bob and Uncle Buster were safely home, although Uncle Bob had been badly wounded, and farm life was good!

The Farm Near Rowan

In March of 1946, it was supposed to be close to spring, but winter was still holding on, cold and windy. At noon, the radio weatherman said it was going to snow again tonight, and Dad looked worried. But Wiggles and I went outside to play anyway, until Mom called me to come in.

"Alice!" Mom said crossly. "Come in the house. Heavens, just look at you! You can't go to town with your hair in such a state. How in the world did you get so much dirt on your head?" and she brushed and brushed until my hair was full of static electricity and stood out on end like a dandelion.

"Wiggles saw a snake in the gravel pit, and we chased it into a hole in the bank, and we dug and dug but it didn't come out," I said. "Ow!" and Mom splashed water on my hair and started braiding it. She made two skinny braids and held me still while she tied a bow at the end of each one. I knew the ribbons would fall off just as soon as I got in the car. My hair was wispy and flew everywhere. The braids were already feeling loose. I was a skinny, blonde kid with fair skin like my mom, but Mom's hair was soft brown and her eyes were pale blue. Mine were green.

"Well, that's the best I can do," sighed Mom. "Go on to the car. I'll be there in a minute. Button your coat!" and she put on her old blue coat and picked up her purse. "We are going to Aunt Bertha's house to get some dahlia bulbs and then we'll pick up Audrey and Janice from choir practice at the church in Rowan."

Aunt Bertha was very proud of her enormous garden. With a lot of help from her sons and Uncle Hugh, she planned it so well that she had flowers blooming year round to decorate the church on Sundays or for local girls' weddings. I wasn't anxious to see her in town. She always asked if I had washed my hands, and why there was dirt on my face. The last time she and Uncle Hugh were at our house for Sunday dinner after church, she told my sisters that sewing on Sunday was a sin. Her knitting needles were clacking away as she spoke. Audrey, always polite, managed not to laugh, and she and Janice quickly moved into the sewing room to work on their latest fabric project. Aunt Bertha kept a close eye on us Hammond Girls.

Aunt Bertha and Uncle Hugh's pretty, white house was at the east end of Main Street, three blocks down from the church, so Mom just ran in to get the sack of bulbs, and we went back to pick up Audrey and Janice where they were waiting on the church steps. Our beautiful white Congregational Church sat on the corner of Main Street and Keith Road, looking out over the block of town businesses. The blacksmith shop was across the street, and the locker plant and the Railroad Depot were at the west end of Main.

Snow began to fall as we started for home. We turned north onto Bingham Street at the saloon, then two blocks up, our three miles of bumpy, gravel road home turned off west at the Methodist church and passed by the new parsonage, then old Mr. Bingham's tiny yellow house and the Nelson place before it crossed the railroad track and ran between cornfields on each side. On to Duffy Hill, where the town kids used to sled in winter, then farther on, we passed the deserted Langdon home where no one had lived for many years, and finally the mailboxes all in a row on the north side of the road at the T intersection, where HAMMOND was neatly printed on the third box from the right.

Two more miles to go! If we turned right, the cemetery was at the junction with the State Highway, but we went left, passing the tree-lined lane to the Duffy farm where my mother was born; across from the Carpenter place which was the original Duffy farm in the 1800's; over the railroad track and the humped-up wooden bridge that my pony hated to cross, to the upper corner of Horse Grove. There, the road made a gentle curve as it descended, crossing the new, white bridge over the Iowa River. The snowflakes were bigger now and falling faster. There's going to be another storm!

After winter was finally over, the river would be up and flooded; the east Slough would be full of dead trees sticking up out of the mud and murky water. The west pastures on each side of the road would have muddy little pools, unless they were completely covered with water. The river was always dark and threatening; none of us kids would risk falling in. Even the fish weren't good to eat – they were mud-cats (catfish). But this day, there was still ice against the banks, with the dark water rushing through the center of the river. It looked scary.

From the hill above the river, we could see our house, and knew whoever was in the kitchen would see us coming. Just a little bit further down and across the bridge, on by the low pasture, and there was the turn into our long lane. Our cattleguards, one at the road and one at the top of the hill into the house and barn yard, were built by our dad and Uncle Buster. When the concrete base was poured for the first one, almost ready for the cross-bars, my sisters and I put our hand prints into the wet cement and etched in the date. When it was done, neither cattle nor horses would cross the guard, knowing instinctively that their hooves would fall through or get caught between the bars, but cars and trucks could drive over without having to bother opening and closing gates.

From that cattle guard, our lane went up hill, past the big cottonwood tree at the first tiny pond, over the pass-through between the gravel pits, up to the second cattleguard, and there we are, home safe before the roads were drifted full of snow.

5

On both sides of that upper cattleguard were big elm trees. On the west side, the fence ran across the bottom of the garden and the lower end of the chicken yard, all the way to the cornfield. On the east, the fence enclosed the metal corn cribs and the hog house. Straight ahead was the lilac bush at the point of the driveway triangle, where, in the summer, I played with the remnants of Janice's old red tricycle, spinning lilac leaves into money like the girl in Rumpelstiltskin.

That grassy triangle in the middle of the driveway separated the barnyard and the house. The space contained the well house and the pole for electricity and telephone wires as well as that big lilac bush. The well house was also a storage room, but the only interesting thing in there was a tanned horse hide that Dad said was from his favorite old horse named Humpy.

The triangle gave visitors a clear direction on where to park. Men coming to talk to my dad about farming, sheep, cows, milk, hogs, corn, or machinery parked on the barn side, since that was where Dad could be found more often than not. The Watkins salesman, the Fuller Brush man, the Creamery truck, and ladies coming for Club or 4-H meetings parked by the house. Folks arriving at or near noon parked anywhere they could squeeze in, because, of course, they would stay for dinner. There was always enough food and room at the table for more people. No one ever went away hungry.

That white, two-story farmhouse was just right for our family of seven, with plenty of room for other extended family members who came to stay for a while, like Mom's sister Betty and Dad's brother Buster. There were three bedrooms, one downstairs where my parents slept, and two large rooms upstairs for the rest of us. The enclosed porch off the parlor was for sewing but it had a fold-out couch where Grammy Hammond slept when she rode the train from Wyoming to Iowa for her annual month-long visits.

In the upstairs, the smaller south room was where Uncle Buster slept when he came to help with the farm work. He had trouble with arthritis, so he didn't visit us in the winter very often. The north room held two double beds and one single bed, a couple of dressers, and a teeny, tiny closet on the south side, with windows on the other three walls. Clothes were shared between sisters, so although the room was full and a little crowded, it was cozy. Hope graduated from high school and went off to college when I was three. Chloe followed her the next year, and they were back and forth from school and work, so there were only three of us girls at home full-time now. When Hope and Chloe were home on weekends, it was always lots of fun. Their friends would be around a lot, and we might go ice skating down on the pond. Chloe always had a boyfriend, Marve, but Hope only went out on double dates. Dad wasn't enthusiastic about them dating.

More Snow, Really?

This morning, it's Saturday, and I'm the only one still in bed. "Girls! Breakfast is almost ready," Mom called. Audrey, Chloe, and Janice were already up and dressed, carrying their shoes as they headed for the stairs. "Get up, lazybones!" and they ran down to the kitchen.

It's hard to get up on mornings when it's still dark and the bedroom windows have an inch of frost on the inside. The upstairs rooms were unheated. The only source of warmth was a vent in the floor of each room so heat could come up from the stove below. Iowa winters are always long and cold, and it seems like March was making winter extra long this year. The hot water bottles we took to bed with us sometimes froze overnight, even with all the quilts on our beds. The quilts were pretty, made with small scraps of cloth from old shirts, dresses, or even feed sacks sewn together to make the quilt top. Then it gets put together with batting in the middle and a flannel back, and the quilting holds it all together and makes it yummy warm. All the women in our family quilted, and we all slept warm. This morning, my cocoon of a blue and white quilt and blankets was toasty, but I was hungry, and I could smell the bacon sizzling downstairs in the kitchen.

Because it was Saturday, everybody would be extra busy, with housework, and getting ready for Sunday School and church tomorrow. But now it was time for me to leap out of bed, grab my clothes and race down the stairs to dress by the stove in the dining room. Yikes! It was freezing!

The pot-bellied stove in the dining room was hot and the corner where I get dressed was warm – but, today, it was already full. Aww, it was a little lamb! Dad must have found the baby when he went out to feed the sheep this morning. It looked too wet and cold to have been born when Dad checked the ewes last night. Silly sheep, to have their babies out in the snowy field instead of the shed in this weather! This poor baby was just lying there in the box on some old towels, all pink and shivering.

"Dad, where did you find the lamb?" I asked. Dad looked tired, and his bright blue eyes were red and watery from the wind and cold outside. I knew that he had been worried about the sheep and must have gone out last night in the storm to check on them.

"This little guy was down by the fence in the pasture late last night. The mother was with him, but it was too cold to leave him out there. He'll warm up pretty quick and I'll take him back to his mother in the shed." Dad said. "I think he'll be ok, but if his mother won't let him nurse, he'll have to be bottle-fed."

I knew what that meant. We had bum lambs every year that needed us to give them bottles of milk. Mom would heat the milk and pour it into clean pop bottles, then put a big black rubber nipple on top. It would be us girls' job to carry the bottles out to the lamb pen and feed the babies. They were always so hungry that sometimes they would pull the nipple right off the bottle and let the milk splatter all over us. The lambs were cute, but it wasn't much fun to have to change clothes and clean our shoes off afterwards, so I hoped that this lamb's mother would take him back and feed him herself.

Breakfast was ready, and Janice brought out grapefruit halves already sectioned with a sharp knife. Audrey carried in the coffee pot and poured Dad's cup full. He squinted up his eyes at the first bite of the grapefruit and put on another spoon of sugar. Then he took a sip of coffee, and Mom said, "Pass your dad the bacon and eggs, please." Breakfast was always good at our house, and today we sat at the table a little longer since it was a winter Saturday. But soon, Dad was on his way out the door again. Chloe went upstairs to start the housework, and Audrey and Janice started the dishes. Mom cleaned the stove and got everything off the table. My job was to put a dust rag on the end of the yardstick and clean under the piano, the couch and the big chair in the parlor.

There was an awful lot to do on Saturdays. We all washed our hair. Chloe, Audrey, and Janice put their hair in pin curls, and Mom rolled mine on rags to make long ringlets. The whole house got swept and dusted, rugs were taken out and shaken, and the linoleum floors were mopped and waxed. If we got our work done in time, we could listen to Let's Pretend on the radio. It was my favorite show. Each week there was a different program; children's stories, fairy tales, or music sponsored by Cream of Wheat. I loved the program, but I didn't eat Cream of Wheat. Yuk!

Of course, there were all the regular chores, too. Dad took care of most of the animals, but we all had outside chores. My jobs were to feed Wiggles, fill the cob pail, and gather eggs from the henhouse, even if some of those old hens liked to peck me. I was always worried that a snake would be in the laying box with the eggs, but there never was. Mom went to the basement to put the milk through the separator, and wash the separator parts afterwards, and she took the chicken feed to the chicken yard and made sure the waterers weren't frozen.

At noon, we ate dinner while listening to the radio; first, the Chicago Stock Report on hog and corn prices, and then One Man's Family. That was Mom's soap opera, and we had to be quiet when it was on. After we ate, Mom mixed up the bread dough for rolls for Sunday dinner, and made two pies because Aunt Bertha and Uncle Hugh would be coming over after church. I had to learn my Bible Verse for Sunday School. Janice and Audrey had homework to do, plus lots of sewing for 4-H or Home Ec. This weekend, Chloe was home from college, so the sewing room was in a flurry; plus., she always had a date with Marvin Smith, the neighbor boy who worked for us in the summers.

Finally, everyone sat down for supper together. Some nights, Dad would tell stories about when he was young. We all wanted to hear his tales, even though sometimes they were a little sad, like the Christmas when he was ten years old. His dad told him he was too old to hang up his stocking. He did it anyway, and on Christmas morning, his stocking had a dried-up chicken bone in it. I thought that was really mean, but Dad laughed. Mostly his stories were pretty funny, or he made them seem funny. We called his mother 'Grammy', and when Grammy came to visit from Wyoming, she had lots of stories, too. Imagine her having ten kids, and seven of them were boys!

Once when she was at our house, Grammy told us, "Well, on our cattle drive, I drove one of the wagons from Douglas, Wyoming to the Montana horse ranch with my four little children. When we got to the Powder River up by old Fort Connor, the government bridge had collapsed and there was dangerous quicksand all around the embankments. But all the horses and wagons made it safely across, and went on to Montana, and your Dad was born in a dugout there the very next year." Grammy was very brave, and her stories were really exciting! It sounded like it would really be fun to have brothers who got into trouble and were real cowboys, instead of sisters who only liked to sew. I sure wished that I had a brother.

That night, after supper when all the evening chores were done, and Marve had come to get Chloe, Dad and Mom had time to sit down and we all listened to *The Bell Telephone Hour* on the radio. The music was wonderful, sometimes with Lily Pons singing opera arias (Mom's favorite) or Gordon MacRay with popular music from "Oklahoma" or "Carousel". Mom sat in the rocking chair by the window to do the mending, and Dad sat by the stove and whittled. He had to go out to check for new lambs before he went to bed, so he kept his coveralls and heavy coat and hat in the kitchen where they would be warm when he put them on. I played on the floor with the old dominos, Lincoln Logs, and marbles, building forts, towns, and roads with a King, Queen, Princess, and soldier marbles, while Janice and Audrey were sewing or working on projects. Janice was teaching herself to tat and make lace, which was pretty, but took a long time and was hard to do.

Dad always went to bed early, but on Saturdays, after my sisters and I went to bed, Mom stayed up to read *The Saturday Evening Post* from cover to cover. She liked to read, and I knew I would, too. I couldn't wait to start school next fall.

Wigglebottom Pee Hammond

One day last January, Uncle Buster drove into our yard in his big hay truck. We had been watching for him all day from the dining room window, because he was always a whirlwind of fun when he visited. Uncle Buster was a little scandalous because he had divorced his second wife and now had a new girlfriend. But he had lots of good stories to tell that made Dad laugh a lot. Uncle Buster's real name was Harold, which he hated, so the family only called him Hal or Buster, the nickname he got as a child when Grammy gave him a Buster Brown haircut, like the boy in the shoe ads on the radio.

This time when Uncle Buster had parked the truck down by the barn, he arrived at the kitchen door and stomped the snow off his boots with a bundle in his arms. " Hi, Girls! I brought you something!" And he laughed and put his package on the floor. The bundle was moving! And then it squeaked! And then, oh, look! It was a puppy!

This wasn't just an ordinary, everyday kind of puppy at all. Oh no! This was a brown and black and tan ball of furry wiggleness, that couldn't wait to kiss us and lick our hands and, oops, pee on the floor! Not even my mother, who was never a fan of house pets or messes or commotions of any kind, had a bad word to say about our new puppy. I think Chloe named him immediately: Wigglebottom Pee Hammond. Welcome to the family!

When he was old enough, Wiggles slept outside on a bale of hay under my parents' bedroom window. But while he was still a baby, he slept in the kitchen corner by the door where Dad piled his outdoor work clothes when he came in the house. One morning after breakfast, Dad went to put his coveralls and mittens back on. When he picked them up, a pancake fell out! Mom had fed Wiggles pancakes left over from breakfast, and after he ate one, he buried the other one in Dad's clothes for a later snack! It was so funny!

Wiggles was a very smart and hardworking farm dog, and he absolutely loved Dad, but he was always ready to play. When he wasn't with Dad working with the cows or sheep, Wiggles and I spent hours together, chasing frogs down at the gravel pits, hunting snakes, or looking for kittens in the hay barn. But work came first, and Wiggles learned his job quickly. His first allegiance was always to my dad, who couldn't call him 'Wiggles' and shortened it to 'Wiggs'. As Wiggs, he learned to guard a gate, round up cows, and herd sheep. When Dad put Wiggs in an open gate or a gap in the fence line and told him to 'stay', the dog didn't move until Dad called him. No animals ever got past him. When a strange vehicle drove into the yard, he barked a warning, but never growled or offered to bite. He was very fierce if varmints ever came near the house and would chase them off immediately, but Mom's geese had him totally buffaloed. They just refused to be herded, and they weren't one bit afraid of him. The first time Wiggles got too close to the big gray gander, he got bit. Geese are fierce.

However, Wiggles did have two very big faults. One was his urge to chase the chickens. We had a lot of chickens and a very big chicken house and fenced yard where the chickens and geese lived. But my mom got some new Bantams, a breed of small, multi-colored chickens. They got picked on by other chickens in the fenced yard, so they escaped under the fence and were always running around on the lawn or out by the garage. They carefully hid their nests and every so often, a hen would show up with a dozen or so of the cutest itty bitty chicks scurrying along behind her. Wiggles could not resist chasing them. The hens squawked and pecked and flapped, but some of the chicks got trampled. And my dad caught him at it. Dad gave poor Wiggles a whipping. Janice and I watched from the sewing room window, and we cried and cried. But Wiggles never chased chickens again.

Wiggles second character failing was chasing cars down on the road. Maybe it was a fun game on days when he was bored, or maybe he just loved to run. Whichever it was, he absolutely had to try to catch cars driving past our farm. Wiggles would watch from the front yard to see a car coming down the hill on the other side of the river. By the time the car crossed the river bridge, Wiggles was on his way down our quarter-mile lane to make the interception when the strange car passed by the end of our driveway. Most days, Wiggles would make the turn and chase for another few yards on the road, but one day it didn't work out very well.

It must have been about supper time, because Dad was in the kitchen and answered the phone. (One black phone, on the wall, party line, long, curly cord.) We heard him say, "Hello, Paul. Oh? Well, I don't think so, but just a minute," and he went to the window. When he came back, he said, "No, he's right outside and looks just fine. Well, I'll call our insurance guy." And hung up. "That was Paul Ketchum," he said. "He called to tell me he was pretty sure he'd killed our dog when it ran out into the road. Made a big dent in the passenger door of his car. Guess he was wrong about it killing Wiggs." But then Dad went outside to check Wiggles over and came back smiling. "Tough dog." Wiggles continued his career of car chasing, but never miscalculated his turn again.

The Garden

Summer work on a farm is never done; you just have to concentrate your efforts on the highest priorities and do what you can. The garden is one of the areas where we could work from dawn to dark every day, and still have plenty to do tomorrow.

Of course, all the planning started just after Christmas. The seed catalogs kept everyone believing that spring would, eventually, arrive following a long, cold, dark winter. The food that grew in the garden would not only feed us all summer but would also be preserved for winter meals. Mom had a college degree, and in addition to teaching in country elementary schools, had taught Home Economics. Once when I asked why we always had such a good breakfast, she said, rather sniffily, "I consider healthy meals to be a part of my education." We were a very healthy family.

This garden planning done in late winter also had to consider the County Fair and 4-H projects. Every third year, the girl's 4H club focused on cooking, and Fair entries would be all kinds of food; fresh, baked, preserved; and decorative. Audrey and Janice were always heavily involved in 4-H, so they took an active part in shopping through the Burpee Seed Brochures. "Susan," Janice said. "Let's order some seeds for gourds. We can dry them and turn them into decorative entries to exhibit at the Fair."

Mom agreed, and added gourds to the list of cucumbers, beets, peas, green beans, squash, melons and pumpkins. All this resulted in packages of seeds arriving with the groceries; seedlings started in paper cups; bare-root plants in a corner on the front porch; mesh bags of gladiola bulbs coming up from the basement; and boxes of surprises in the mail. We would know it was truly spring when a box of live chicks was waiting for us at the Post Office in town.

When spring finally did come and it was time to go to work, everyone helped. First, the garden had to be disced and raked as soon as the ground thawed and dried enough to work. Last fall, Dad had hooked the plow to the small tractor and turned over all the vegetable remains and the dirt to mix in the manure fertilizer. Now, after the raking had smoothed out the ground, he and Mom would stake out lines with string, marking the rows. Once the preparation work was done, Dad went back to the fieldwork, and didn't have much time to help in the garden; but he did plant lots of sweet corn and popcorn in the field just north of the house.

Weeding that huge garden was a chore that nobody liked but had to be done. Any summer punishment was almost always "hoe a row'. Mom did more of the weeding when Audrey and Janice were detasseling, and I helped a little bit, too, But the garden thrived. Items that looked extra good or really big went to the County Fair to vie for ribbons, both in the 4-H exhibits and in the general categories. But mostly, we ate, canned, and froze a huge amount of fruit and vegetables.

The strawberry patch was the only thing that didn't need much preparation or maintenance work. The plants survived winter with a light covering of straw. Once that was removed, the white blossoms began showing up, and very soon after, we had ripe red strawberries ready to pick. We had strawberries with cream, on cereal, in shortcake, in ice cream, jams, preserves, whipped cream pies, and as topping for angel food cakes. All the extra berries went to the freezer for winter feasts. Mom said the reason our strawberries were so good, was the little green striped garter snake that lived in the berry patch. She protected that terrible reptile fiercely, and Wiggles and I were absolutely forbidden to "bother" her snake, or chase it, or bark at it, or scream when we saw it. Mom's claim was that the snake ate all the bugs that might endanger her strawberries. If that was true, no wonder that snake was so content to live in that one particular area. If he patrolled the entire patch for bugs, he surely would have doubled his body weight in a week. Maybe he invited his entire family in to join him for the spring bug migration. Who knows? I never saw more than one snake in that patch, and Mom had a wonderful strawberry crop   every   year.

Geese in the Gravel Pit

Mom raised geese. She sold the adult geese for Thanksgiving or Christmas dinners or as breeding pairs; sold the goslings to raise; and also sold eggs to the Hatchery in Clarion.

Her geese spent their nights in the chicken house at the top of the fenced chicken yard, safe from foxes, weasels, or other varmints. The yard was big, giving the chickens a big area to run – we had free-range before it was 'in'. There were huge old sycamore trees at the top of the yard in front of the chicken house, then a grove of black locust trees at the south end. Every morning, Mom would go down below the garden to open the south gate and the geese would march out of the yard in single file, heading for the gravel pit ponds where they swam, ate frogs, grazed in the grass, and watched our driveway to honk at strangers. In the evening, the geese would file back up the hill to be safely tucked in for the night.

In the spring, the geese began to nest, and almost always chose sites near the old gravel pits now full of water. There were four ponds, with another tiny little pond near the road. A marshy area sometimes had water but was mostly full of weeds, frogs, and mosquitoes. The biggest pond was reportedly bottomless to keep me careful near it, but Audrey and Janice had put together a rickety raft. I was never brave enough to try using it, so it became a favorite nesting spot for the geese. Once the eggs were laid, the female never left the eggs alone, and if her hisses and wing flaps didn't scare off an intruder, her gander mate would take on anyone or anything that got too close.

It did happen that once in a while a nest was raided or the goose died or was injured and couldn't do the hatching. The eggs might end up in the "deep well" of our kitchen stove. It was, in effect and purpose, a built-in crock pot. Mom would turn it on warm, line it with an old towel, then carefully put in the eggs. We would all wait anxiously for the first cracks to appear. Those babies were so darn cute! Chartreuse little critters would chirp and waddle around the kitchen looking for food or their Mom. We called them "doppies" because they were so adorable.

Adult geese are big; they are fierce; they are extremely territorial; and they poop everywhere! Having them down at the gravel pits was good – if someone drove up the lane, geese would honk and alert the dog. Wiggles avoided the geese after an unfortunate misunderstanding that left him with a bloody nose. Yet they didn't fare so well with Grammy. My Grammy was a sturdy, no-nonsense woman, strong and hard-working, who put up with no guff. A big, fierce, grey gander was misguided enough to hiss and then try to bite her when she got too close; Grammy snatched up that goose and had his neck wrung and head chopped off lickety split. My mother was definitely not pleased to lose her big gander There might have been a few snickers in private, but nobody said a word to Grammy or Mom. The unlucky gander went into the freezer, and roast goose would be on the menu for Thanksgiving dinner that year.

On Easter Break, Chloe brought her college roommate home to visit. Jojo, Josephina Manresa, was a city girl from the Philippines. Life on our farm was shockingly alien to her, but she was a good sport and joined in feeding lambs, and watched the milking. She laughed at the cats getting squirted with milk, but wasn't fond of the barnyard smells.

The weather north of us had been very rainy, so the river was out of its banks and flooding the river bottom pasture. Over the next few days, the water kept rising until it covered the entire field and was getting closer and closer to the barn. On that evening, when Mom went down to open the gate for the geese to come into the chicken yard, the geese were nowhere to be found! What happened? Where are they? They had swum away on the flood water   and   were   gone.

It was The Great Goose Chase. The whole family came out to search for the flock. Audrey drove Chloe and Jojo up to the Hilltop bridge over the river just north of us. We called the neighbors, Carpenters, Ketchums, and Knuts, to see if the geese had been spotted. Dad got the horse and rode south towards Horse Grove and Bingham Woods. Uncle Buster was no help; he got his fishing pole and caught a great big catfish right down below the barn. Chloe and Jojo came back wet and tired from walking the river bank and avoiding snakes, but still having fun. Even without finding any trace of the missing geese, it ended up a party, with the neighbors pitching in and somehow there was a bonfire and hot dogs and marshmallows and hot chocolate.

To everyone's relief, the geese sailed home on the river and arrived back at their gate all safe and sound the very next day.

The Big Red Barn

I thought our three-story barn was huge, but it was really just an ordinary sized farm building with faded, shabby red paint. The weather vane on the roof had been shot so many times from the front porch of the house before we lived there and the bullet holes destroyed so much of it, that we couldn't really tell what it had been when it was new. The barn's west ground floor held the milking stalls, where the Jersey cows, Missy, Old Mama, Daisy, Lucy, Bessie, and Gert, lined up in front of the door every day at 6 AM and 6 PM. Daisy was my favorite. She was friendly, curious, and willing to be petted. Each cow had her very own stall in the milk room. Woe betide the foolish one who put her head into the wrong feed manger, and poor Bessie, who was a little flighty and maybe not very smart, was usually the one who caused the problems. There would be total cow chaos! All the cows would be confused and nervous, mooing, pushing, and crowding around to try to find their rightful space; and my dad would have to wade into the roiling mass of moo-cows to establish order again. It's not good to upset cows. In a melee like that, even the cats would be jumpy, scattering into the hay mow or the feed mangers to avoid being stepped on while waiting for their pan of milk. But Dad could say, "Sooo cows, sooo cows. Here Bessie. Wait, Daisy. Go, Lucy," and get the cows calm and back into the proper order. Then he'd set up the milking stool; fill up the cat pan with warm milk; and get the buckets of milk up to the house to run through the separator. On the days when the cows were upset, there was less milk than usual.

The upper story of the barn was full of baled hay, put in during the fall and used all winter as feed for milk cows, horses, and beef cattle. The cats were happy to use the stacked hay as their own maternity ward. At almost any time of the year, we could crawl around among the hay bales to find batches of kittens. Hay bales were not huge round ones. They were rectangular, tied with either baling wire or baling twine, and weighed between 40 and 60 pounds, depending on the type of hay (alfalfa or prairie). When the bales were stacked in the barn, there were spaces deliberately left between the bales here and there to prevent spontaneous combustion that made perfect cubby holes for Mama cats to hide in and for me to crawl through to find them.

The whole back of the barn was lower ground level where there was an open shed with a large feed manger for the cattle or sheep to shelter and be fed during storms or high drifted snow. The old milk room next to the shed was just used for storage, but was a great hunting ground for the cats to catch mice.

The horse stalls were in between the new milk barn and the hay loft. Pal and Cub, the team of work horses, were gone now, but Dad's saddle horse, Jinx, and my pony, Lady, lived in those stalls during the winter. Dad loved horses and liked making trades and deals, so other horses came and went, trading with Uncle Elden, Uncle Buster, or from the Sale Barn at Belmond. We always had a horse to ride. Dad rode to move or check on the Hereford cattle, round up sheep, or look for the milk cows. He was always a cowboy at heart.

All these animals, cows, horses, sheep, and hogs, produced a lot of waste, which had to be cleared out of the barn daily. All that poop got shoveled into an enormous heap in the barnyard corner, and in the winter it all froze, which kept down the odor. In the spring the manure pile, plus all the chicken house poop, would be shoveled into the manure spreader. Dad would hook up the old John Deere tractor to the spreader and haul the manure out to the garden and fields to be plowed into the ground as fertilizer. That was one job that never fell to Mom or any of us girls.

The barnyard front fence ran from the barn over to the grainery. That building was divided into the oats and corn bins on one side, and the cob house on the other side. The oats and corn were for the horses and cattle, and the dry corn cobs were used as fuel or fire starters in the house stoves; the kitchen trash-burner, and the pot-bellied stove in the dining room. The cobs stayed dry in the cob house and were used all winter. It was my job to take the basket and fill it up with those stickery red cobs for the stoves.

When Dad picked corn in the fall, the corn still on the cob that didn't go into the tall wire corn cribs was shelled by a machine with a long chute at the end. First the chute aimed into the corn bin next to the cob house until it was full, then the chute was redirected to fill up wagons that went to the Rowan Elevator to be sold when the price was right, according to the Chicago Stock Report. Corn husks went to feed the hogs, and the cobs were shoveled into the cob house to dry. Nothing was wasted. Nothing.

Aunt Betty's Wedding

At the supper table, Mom said, "Girls, Betty is getting married and we are all invited. And she would like to have Audrey sing *"Always"* at the ceremony." Audrey turned pink and said she'd love to do it. We were all very excited – well, maybe not Dad. He knew a wedding meant wearing a suit and being out of the fields when work needed to be done.

Aunt Betty was Mom's youngest sister, only a little older than my oldest sister Hope, and we all liked her a lot. She had stayed at our house off and on while she went to college, always happy and fun to be around, but she had been teaching this last year and staying at Aunt Dolly's house near Clarion. We didn't know her husband-to-be, but Mom said he was a farmer from Jewell, where Betty had been teaching. He was a Veteran and had served in WWII, so Dad and Uncle Bob both approved of him.

When Aunt Bertha heard the news about Aunt Betty's marriage, she was very upset. "What is she thinking? How can it ever work out? The man is a Lutheran!" (We were Congregationalists.)

But nobody else seemed to be worried, and we Hammond girls sure didn't care. Audrey worried a little bit because she was scared to sing all alone; but mostly, we concentrated on what we would wear. Chloe found a pattern and chose pale blue fabric, Audrey had time to make me a new dress, blue and white striped, since she was going to wear her gold formal to sing, and Janice decided to wear the pale green coat-dress she had made this spring for the 4-H style show. It was too bad that Hope had classes and couldn't go with us.

When Aunt Betty's big day came, we were all dressed up and ready to leave for the wedding. Just before we got in the car, Mom gave me a pair of white, crocheted gloves just like the ones she was wearing. Oh, they were beautiful! They went perfectly with my new dress. I felt as elegant as a movie star!

The Clarion Congregational Church (which Aunt Bertha approved of, thank goodness) was packed full of family and friends. Betty looked beautiful in her long, white wedding dress, with a lace veil covering her blonde hair. Our new Uncle Don had a rose from her bouquet in his lapel and looked nervous, but I greatly admired his bright red hair.

Even though she had been practicing for weeks, Audrey was so nervous that her voice shook a little as she started, "I'll be loving you, Always." But nobody else really noticed. The song made all the women in the church get teary-eyed and reach for a hankie.

After the ceremony, everyone went downstairs to the reception in the church basement. Aunt Betty's red rose bouquet tied with long blue ribbons was decorating the refreshment table where Mom and her other three sisters, Millie, Cleo, and Dolly, were serving slices of cake and Uncle Bob's wife, Wilma, was pouring coffee. All our family was there, of course; Uncle Joe, Aunt Bertha and Uncle Hugh, Howard and Ethel, and all the Duffys, right down to Charles and me, the two youngest Duffy cousins.

The older cousins never wanted to have anything to do with us younger ones, so I was surprised when three of the older girls, Kathy, Marilyn and Linda, came over to me. I had just finished eating my piece of wedding cake and was wondering if I could go through the line again for more, or if Aunt Cleo would catch me and tell Mom. The three girls had been whispering together on the other side of the room. As they approached, Linda looked a little scared and kept looking over her shoulder to see if her mother, Aunt Dolly, was watching. Then, Kathy said to me, with a sly smile, "Did you know your sisters aren't really your sisters?"

I was astonished! Why would she say such a dumb thing? "Of course they're my sisters!" I replied, huffily. "They're half sisters because we have different mothers."

Kathy seemed disappointed. "Well," she snapped, "I bet you didn't know that their mother died because a rattlesnake bit her."

That was so silly that it made me laugh right out loud! Just because my dad was a cowboy from Wyoming and all four of my sisters were born there didn't mean they were overrun with rattlesnakes! I said, "Their mom just got sick and died; there wasn't any stupid snake."

Kathy got mad that I laughed, but I didn't care and went off to get another piece of cake when Aunt Cleo wasn't looking.

Honestly, that Kathy! Of course, I had always known that we were a three-sided family. When my sisters' mother died in Wyoming, Dad brought them to Iowa because most of her family lived here. That's how Dad met my Mom, because she lived across the river from the Hiams land where Dad was farming.

And the three sides of family are why we had so darn many relatives!

Hay Days

In mid-summer, it was haying time, and that meant Dad was worried about the weather. The alfalfa hay was ready to harvest, but the weatherman on WHO radio was predicting rain next week. The question was whether to trust the weather forecast and try to get the hay mowed, raked, dried, baled and into the barn and haystacks in five days. Could we do it? Was the weather man right? If the rain came earlier than expected, would it rot the hay?

Dad and Mom talked about it, and then Dad called our neighbor, Paul Ketchum. "Paul, it's Earl Hammond. Will you be able to start haying this week? I'm thinking I'll mow today, and rake the day after tomorrow, so we should be able to bale on Friday. Radio says rain on Sunday, so I'm hoping to get done by Saturday night. When are you planning to start your fields?"

After some more conversation, they agreed that Paul would bring his baler and help with the baling and stacking, and he would bring along Bob Ketchum, his nephew. Dad already had high school boys, Marve Smith and Chester Judd, lined up to work, so he was satisfied there would be enough hands to get the work done quickly. He told Mom that she could plan on having the haying crew to feed on Friday and Saturday, and she started making a list for the grocery store.

Throughout the summer, there were morning 'lunches' going out to the fields around 9:30 am, then huge noon dinners at 12:00 sharp, and afternoon 'lunches' around 3:00 again to keep workers fueled up and hydrated. With 4 extra men, it would mean more food and drinks to prepare and carry out. Mom always had extra food and drinks on hand anyway, just in case other folks showed up to help or to see what was going on. Uncle Joe and Herb Ketchum, Paul's dad, were often out at our place or at Paul's. The 'lunch' in the morning and again in the afternoon needed to include a 20 gallon cream can of ice cold water or sweetened tea, a wash pan with warm water and towels, and substantial cookies or cake, like brownies or coffee cake. All worked hard and needed both the rest break and the food and drinks to keep working efficiently.

Summer weather in Iowa was hot, so dehydration was a real concern. Dad wore long-sleeved work shirts, jeans, and always, a hat. By the end of September, his hands and face were heavily tanned, but his forehead and arms were still pale white in a "Farmer's Tan". When Mom worked outside in the garden or driving a tractor in the field, she wore a huge hat, one of Dad's long-sleeved shirts, jeans and a ton of Pond's Cold Cream on her face and neck. Even then, she got freckles. Both Marve and Chester sometimes worked without a shirt, but were careful to put it back on when any of us girls were around. Our parents had very strict rules about "boys".

Dad went out to start the mowing, and we heard the new John Deere tractor start up as he headed out to the hay field. It would be hot and dirty work, and he would be more than ready for dinner at noon. He would need a glass of ginger ale, too, to ease his stomach ache. Mom kept a bottle in the refrigerator just for him since the doctor said it would help his ulcer..

By Friday, the hay had been mowed, let dry for a day then raked into windrows, and was ready for baling. The weather had stayed hot and dry just as the weatherman on the radio had predicted. Dad listened to the news every night to get the weather report, and both he and Mom watched the sky for rain clouds. So far, it was good haying days.

We didn't have a baler so we waited for Paul to arrive with his machinery. The Ketchums lived just across the west field, and Paul and Dad traded work back and forth when they needed help. Paul had to bring the tractor and baler around by the road since our hay field was in the 80 acres of river bottom part of the farm. Bob, Marve, and Chester were all ready to go to work, and Mom had started cooking the day before. There was a big batch of raisin and walnut cookies in the cupboard, and roll dough was rising on the back of the stove. We would have a big pork roast, with potatoes, gravy, warm rolls, carrots, jello salad with chopped apples and walnuts, corn on the cob, and rhubarb pie for dinner today. Yum, yum! Bob Ketchum was famous for how much corn he could eat; his nickname was 'Corn Cob.'

The machinery arrived, and the men went to the field. The baler, pulled by Paul's big red tractor, started at the first windrow, and gobbled up the hay as it drove along. The hay went in the front of the machine, was compacted into a rectangle about 18 inches by 40 inches, then tied with baling twine and spit out the back onto the ground. This year, the hay had grown thick, so the windrows were high and bales processed through the machine at a faster rate. Paul drove the big tractor, and Dad drove our John Deere pulling the flat-bed trailer along behind. Bob, Marve, and Chester were on the ground behind the baler, and as bales came out of the machine, picked them up and stacked them on the trailer. Since the hay was thick, the bales filled up the trailer quickly. Then the two boys would drive it back to the barn and off-load the bales onto the elevator belt that took them up into the hay loft of the barn. They had to hurry, so they didn't get too far behind the baler, but by noon, there was almost half the field already done with bales waiting on the ground to be picked up.

The men welcomed the morning break in the field with water and cookies while they rested for a few minutes, but at noon they came back to the house for dinner. Mom had set up a trestle table on sawhorses outside in the shade, with a washstand and towels for them to wash up. Mom and I carried out the dishes of food, and everyone filled their plates and dug in. When the food was gone, the boys laid down for a quick nap in the shade while Dad and Paul chatted. Paul smoked, which Dad said wasted time, but they had a rest, then were ready to go back to work. More of the same all afternoon, and by dusk, Paul and Bob had gone home and it was time for evening chores.

Saturday morning, Dad was watching the sky nervously. It was cloudy and the air smelled like rain. "Need to hurry," Dad said. "Hope Paul can get started right away." And he was out the door to collect Marve and Chester. Mom was worried about the hay. If the bales got wet, they couldn't go into the barn. Wet hay bales could burst into flames all by themselves, and we sure didn't want that!

Working hard, the men filled the hay loft in the barn, and started the hay stack in the pasture just below the hog house. Dad was very particular about how the bales were stacked because he didn't want it all to fall over if the cows ate some hay from the bales on the sides. The stack began with a row of bales on their sides, tight against each other to make the base. Then the next rows went on with the bales flat, facing alternate directions. Marve and Chester worked hard at the haystack, while Bob and Dad picked up the hay in the field and brought it back to them. Paul was done baling by noon, and went home after dinner but Bob stayed on to help finish up.

Just as the last load of hay bales was arriving at the new stack, it began to sprinkle. Marve threw the last bale up to Chester on the top of the pile as the rain came down in earnest, and the boys whooped and ran for the gravel pit. They splashed into the pond, scattering geese and snapping turtles, and Wiggles was happy to join   them.

Dad and Mom were happy that the hay was safe, and there would be plenty of food for the cattle and horses all next winter. The new hay smelled wonderful, and the barn cats had a lovely new place to have their kittens.

Magic in the Pasture

I never had an imaginary friend. I didn't need one. I had sisters and cousins, cats and chicks, a pony, and Wiggles. All summer I was busy exploring the farm, doing a few chores, riding Lady through the fields, climbing trees, and playing in the gravel pits.

In our home, time to do nothing was a luxury for the grown-ups. One hot day, when the adults were all working from dawn to well past dark in the fields and my sisters were concentrating on their 4-H projects, I found a magic spot down by the east side gravel pits.

Three young cottonwood trees grew in a three-sided configuration, making a space about five feet wide with thick grass covering the floor of the triangle. The branches of each tree brushed the tops of their neighbors, to keep the little space shady in the hot summer sun. The big pond where the geese and snapping turtles swam was on one side, and the little pond by the road was just a few yards away. The cornfield on the other side of the fence ran all the way down to the river. Animals usually grazed in this small pasture and drank at the ponds, but there was never any animal poop in that little patch of grass. It was never weedy, and the grass was always cropped as close as if it were a lawn. While it was in plain sight of the road, our lane, and the house, it was still my secret place. It was magic.

If any place was going to be special, it should have been Little Pond by the road. That huge, old cottonwood tree bent out over the bank and its roots and the climbing rocks made perfect places to sit and dangle my feet in the water. The water was clear and cool. It was where Wiggles and I played, chasing frogs, catching tadpoles, and splashing water everywhere. It was a good spot for fun, but it definitely wasn't magic.

My magic spot had room for just me and Wiggles. I kept some pretty rocks in a hollow beside the roots of the biggest tree. Sometimes I would bring some of my favorite paper dolls with me and make up adventures for them. Those dollies and I took some exciting trips, usually traveling to places only seen in the pages of the *National Geographic* magazines that were stacked up on the stairs going up to our bedroom. Africa and Alaska were our favorite places to visit because of the wild animals. Lions and tigers and bears! Safaris, Zulu tribes, glaciers, and Inuits: all of them fascinated me.

Wiggles never stayed there long. When I was busy with the dolls, he lost interest and left to look for snapping turtle, chase snakes, or swim in whichever pond the geese weren't in. I could lie in that lush grass and daydream until I heard someone calling me.

Nothing strange or unexpected ever happened in that spot, so it's hard to explain how I discovered it was magic or why I was so sure that it was. It was just very quiet and peaceful, and all mine for just that one summer. Who knew that as an adult, I would actually live in North Africa and Alaska? Was it Magic?

Uncle Joe's Joke

A baby goat arrived at our house late one evening in the back seat of Uncle Joe's old black car. Uncle Joe was a family friend as well as a relative-by-marriage, an old man who now lived alone in town close to the highway. He didn't talk much, but always had candy corn in the pocket of his Sunday suit for me. He was often at the sale barn with other retired farmers, sometimes to sell his hogs, but sometimes just to see and visit with other farmer friends. On this day, the sale barn auctioneer had run a little white and gray kid into the ring as a joke, and Uncle Joe ended up with the highest bid of $1. He thought it would be funny for my dad to have the goat, so he brought it to our house, dropped it off at our doorstep, and roared away again in his old car without a word to anyone.

Well, it was a pretty good joke. The little guy was really cute and after we all finished petting him and praising his sweet little face, Dad couldn't very well send him away. So, we named the baby goat Johnny, and he became my friend, playmate, and transportation around the farm for the rest of the summer.

Uncle Buster was staying with us just then, as he was between wives at the time. Of course, there was no discussion of his second divorce(!) in front of us girls, but, of course, we knew. First Evelyn and now Georgia! Scandalous! Uncle Buster was good looking and could be very charming; he, along with Dad, was one of those handy Hammond men who could make or fix about anything. He decided to build me a small goat cart. Then Dad found some old pieces of leather straps hanging in the garage, and the two brothers put together a complete harness for the goat and taught him to pull that cart with me in it.

My maiden voyage of the cart did not go well. I was not experienced at driving a wagon. Johnny Goat had never before seen a wagon, let alone pulled one that was tied on behind him. The first time around the farmyard triangle with Dad watching was fine. Johnny and I were quite pleased with ourselves, and with an overabundance of confidence, decided to go down the lane.

It must have been the cattle guard that caused the problem. Johnny was moving along quickly, the cart and I following properly, until we hit the cattle guard. Johnny jumped, the cart jerked forward, and I shrieked and howled.

All Johnny knew to do was RUN, and he ran full out. We went down the lane, took a quick left turn, made another right turn, and ended up with Johnny, the cart, and me in the gravel pit pond with the startled geese.

I was safe in the cart, except we were surrounded by water. Still crying, I was saved by Marve, who was our summer hired hand. He rescued me, pulled the goat out of the water and salvaged the cart, all before Dad or Uncle Buster got there. He was a Hero!

Poor Johnny! He continued to grow up and get into more trouble. He hopped up on Aunt Betty's car, ground to hood to roof, and made some scratches. He tried to play chase with Wiggles when there was dog-work to be done. As his horns began to grow in, he tried to challenge cars driving into the yard. And finally, the last straw: Mom planted a Buckeye Sycamore tree by the back door, and Johnny ate the sapling right down to the root.

Johnny went away. He didn't go back to the sale barn, but went instead to Aunt Dolly's house, where he became Dad's joke on Uncle Elden. But Johnny lived happily ever after, running with the ponies and milk cows on their farm.

Cats, Cats, Cats!

Mama Kitty was looking suspiciously thin when I was down in the milk barn that evening. "Dad, have you seen any kittens in the hay barn?" I asked. We had lots of barn cats, but Mama Cat always had the nicest kittens and was willing to let me pet her.

Dad squirted another stream of milk towards the cat pan from where he was milking Daisy and said he hadn't exactly been looking for kittens while he was forking hay down to the cattle in the shed. Well, of course not. Dad worked hard and didn't have time to hunt kittens. But I knew who had time and would like to help me with a hunt – Wiggles! He was always up for a search through the bales of hay piled in the barn loft. Tomorrow's project was all set.

The next morning after chores were done, Wiggles and I got into the hay loft through the horse stalls, going up over the mangers and crawling past the half-wall into the hay loft. Wiggles needed no help at all to get over the mangers or wall. He was thrilled to be on a quest, even though I'm not sure he knew what exactly we were looking for.

Hay is dusty and scratchy, the smell of it made my nose itch, and after a few minutes of climbing up the stacked bales, the dust and hay particles were in my clothes and in Wiggles' fur. It didn't take long for us to start sneezing, but we were determined to find – well, I was determined to find - kittens, and Wiggles was along for the fun of it.

We were almost at the top of the piled bales, getting close to the roof of the barn when I spotted it. There it was; a good space between bales with a tunnel going towards the inner pile. Cat hair was rubbed against one edge of the tunnel, which meant frequent traffic in and out. Kittens! I was sure of it.

Only one thing was holding me back from that tunnel: snakes. When the baler went through the field gathering up the hay in the windrows, packing it into rectangular bales, and then binding them with twine, it would occasionally also gather up a snake with the hay and include it in the bale. I don't like snakes. I especially don't like having one appear unexpectedly. Wiggles, on the other hand, loved snakes to surprise him, or to surprise them himself. So, on a kitten hunt, our plan was for Wiggles to put his head into the tunnel to check for snakes. If he went crazy, there was a snake inside. If he yelped and backed out quickly, the Mama cat was in there, fiercely guarding her babies. If he sniffed and was cautiously interested, it meant kittens. If he just pulled his head back out and waited for further instructions, it meant "there's nothing going on in here so let's go somewhere else."

Yay! This time we were lucky on three counts: there was no snake, Mama Cat wasn't in the tunnel, and there were five itty bitty kitties in a cozy nest. One was grey, one black, two were black and white, and the sweetest little baby was a calico. Orange, black, white, and a touch of grey were her colors, so adorable. I knew she was a girl because all calico cats are girls, and it was love at first sight. I named her Callie and decided to take her back to the house to live with me as soon as she was old enough to leave her mother.

The next day when I went back to visit Callie, there were no kittens in the nest. Mama Cat must have moved them to a safer place somewhere else in the barn. Unless we could find the new hiding spot, I would have to wait until Mama Cat brought her babies out to drink milk in the milking barn to find sweet Callie again.

Wiggles was joyful to have another hunt going on. We climbed all around the hay bales, getting more and more hay in our outer coverings, and sneezing more and more often. We went all the way up to the roof and back down to the lower cattle shed. No luck. I was sad, thinking that Callie would not remember me by the time she was old enough to go to the milk barn. But maybe she would; I'd just have to wait and see.

Dad promised he would watch out for the new kittens to show up at milking time, so that made me feel better. Dad never had time to play with kittens or even pet the cats, but I knew that it made him laugh to watch them catch the milk he squirted from the cow towards the cat pan. He knew it was important to have cats in the barnyard to keep the mice out of the corn and oats that we needed to feed our cows and horses. So I waited.

One evening, maybe a month later, while we were eating supper, Dad said, "Didn't you want to find a calico kitten awhile back?"

"Oh, yes!" I said and was so excited that I dropped my fork and Mom frowned. "Have you seen her?"

"Well, there was a calico at the cat pan tonight. It'll probably be back tomorrow."

At last! Tomorrow, I would find Sweet Callie, and bring her up to the house. Mom would surely let me keep her with me; well, maybe she would. It was worth a try.

But although Mom liked cats, she didn't want Callie to live in the house. I was disappointed, but it was OK with Callie. She came in to play and eat extra snacks, look around for mice, but then was ready to go back to the barn. She knew she had work to do and she was a fierce predator on rodents.

Callie had several litters of kittens over the next few years, and taught them all to follow her good example catching mice, but there were no more calico kittens. And, alas, eventually Callie went the way of all barn cats; she didn't show up for milk from the cat pan any more. And there was never another calico cat born in the barn.

Where the Tall Corn Grows

"Mom, the corn is too high," I complained late that hot summer afternoon. My hair was plastered to my head and sweat ran down my back. Even with both windows open, the kitchen was steaming hot. There were peaches and Mason jars on every flat surface in the room, plus there were two bushel-baskets of the fuzzy yellow fruit waiting to be peeled and canned. The floor was sticky and the smell of sugary peaches was heavy.

"Where have you been?" Mom asked. She looked tired, and was as sweaty as I was, and her dress and apron had spatters of peach syrup all down the front. "I thought you were riding the pony."

"I was. That mean old Lady almost rubbed me off on the barbed wire fence in the pasture! And then she kept trying to go back to the barn. But I made her go through the gate to the cornfield and then she started to run down the corn row!" I caught my breath and stomped my foot. "We were in the corn and it was so big I couldn't see where we were and I got kind of scared and Lady was really running." And a little sob almost got out. But Mom was so busy that she didn't notice. "I wanted to go down to Ketchum's to see what Bernie is doing, but we were running the wrong way."

Lady was a part-Shetland pony, at least twice as old as me. She was hard headed and had very definite ideas about where to go and when it was appropriate for me to go along. Catching her when she was in the pasture was a long process, involving chasing her with the bridle held behind my back and a coffee can of oats or shelled corn held out as a bribe to let me get close enough to grab her halter. She never came when I whistled, like Trigger when Roy Rogers called him, although Dad could always walk right up to her. She also tried to bite me or step on my foot if I wasn't paying attention. Since everybody knew her tricks with teeth and hoofs, there was no sympathy for the injured one, always me.

"Look out!" Mom said, crossly. "These jars are ready to come out of the canning kettle, and they're hot! Did you water Lady and put her back in the pasture?" Hot water dripped onto the linoleum as she lifted the jars full of beautiful peach halves out of the kettle and put them on the cooling rack. I knew that when we heard the lids 'pop', it meant that the seal was good and the peaches would be safe to eat next winter. All the cooled jars would go to the basement and sit on shelves with the tomatoes, apples, beans, beets, peas, pickles, jams, jellies, and apple butter that would feed us until summer came around again.

I nodded yes, I had taken care of Lady, and sat on the kitchen stool to watch as Mom put six more jars of peaches into the boiling kettle and set the timer. Then she wiped her face with her apron and said, "There! That's the last batch today, thank goodness. Let's have a glass of iced tea, and when these jars come out, we'll take some tea out to your dad. Then I can get this awful mess cleaned up and start some supper. Get a lemon and an orange out of the icebox and roll them for juice while I make the tea." She put a pot of water on to heat, and reached for the tea box in the cupboard. Then she pulled open the bin where the 50 pound bag of sugar was kept and put a cupful in the glass gallon jar. I rolled and rolled the lemon and orange until the fruit felt squishy. Mom sliced them up and put them in the jar. Then she cooled the hot tea with some cold water and a big chunk of ice, and poured it into the big   jar.

I was happy to have a glass of cool tea – what a treat! And I was also happy that supper would probably be potato soup, because that's what Mom usually cooked on canning days.

Mom packed the basket with cookies, a wet washcloth, a towel, and the tin camping cups. After the last peaches came out of the kettle, I got to carry the basket and Mom carried the big jar of tea. We walked down to the garden gate, past the gravel pit and the old shack, to the tree at the alfalfa field fence. We could hear the tractor at the other side of the field. Dad was raking the cut alfalfa into windrows to cure, getting ready for baling. The alfalfa smelled really good, but it made my nose itch. The tractor was going around the field and pretty soon it was coming towards us. Dad raised his hand to say he'd seen us, and the green and yellow John Deere tractor gave a couple loud 'PoPs' as it slowed and stopped.

Dad got off the tractor and took off his hat to wipe his head as he came into the shade. He stretched and rubbed his back, then took the washcloth and cleaned his hands and face. "Pretty hot today," he said, as Mom poured tea into his cup. "That's sure good. It hits the spot!"

"The hay looks good," Mom said as she handed out the cookies. "Do you think you'll get done before the rain?"

"Should be, if we don't break down. Marve and Chester will be here to help on Wednesday."

"Oh, that's good. I need to get some baking done before they get here, and maybe you could kill a couple chickens in the morning before you go back to the field again. Those boys sure can eat! Is Chester staying through corn picking?" Mom asked.

"Yes, he'll go home to start school a little late. He's good help and there's plenty of work to do here." Dad replied.

"Dad!" I said. "Lady tried to rub me off on the barbed wire fence today. She's really mean sometimes."

"Yes," Mom said, "and the corn is too high, right?" and she looked amused. "Was it as high as an elephant's eye?" and Dad snorted.

"Yeah," I said gloomily, "I didn't go to Ketchum's like I wanted to. Dumb old pony!" I grumbled, and ate another cookie.

"Time to get back to work," Dad announced, still laughing. "Thanks for the lunch. And don't worry, the corn will be ready to pick before long, and you'll be able to see where you're going." As he drove the tractor back into the field, Mom packed everything up and gave me the basket. We trudged back to the kitchen, still hot and   steamy   and   smelling   of   peaches.

The Parlor

The Parlor, or the Front Room, was seldom used or heated unless we had visitors: Marve Smith, Chloe's boyfriend, who came to pick her up when they had a date; the preacher who came for dinner after church on Sunday; the Duffy dinners when all the families gathered; 4-H meetings when it was our turn to host; and several winters of Card Club, where the neighbors came over to play '500'.

The room was a good size. There was a carpet on the wood floor, and there was a space between the edges of the rug and wall where the dust mop just fit on Saturday cleanings. The piano was on the bare floor but the piano stool was on the carpet, which was a faded blue, with a pattern of muted flowers.

The formal front door and picture window were facing the walnut tree and hedges to the north, but only strangers would have used that entry. Knocking there would have resulted in a long wait, and exclamations of "who could that be?" and a jerk and creak as the door was pulled open. Everyone in farm country knew to go to the kitchen door.

The parlor was where the "good" furniture was. In addition to the piano, there was a large, odd, home-made, walnut chair with stiff green cushions that no one ever sat in, and then the obligatory set of matching couch and chair. This set, which was a Christmas gift from my dad to my mom when I was a baby, was covered in dark red, itchy, and indestructible upholstery. The fabric had a raised pattern that if stroked one way, was a lighter color than the other way. The furniture was so heavy that it took two people to move it, so spring cleaning was the only time there was any rearranging done. One of my chores was to dust under those red monsters, using a rag tied on the end of The Yardstick.

About that yardstick: It was the equivalent of a nuclear bomb in the event of misbehavior. It lived on the top of the doorframe between the kitchen and dining room. I don't remember that it was ever actually used; just the tone of voice in the threat of it being taken down was enough. "Lord, help the blind!" was the warning signal, and was the closest my mother ever came to swearing.

Those heavy, red pieces of furniture were fine for establishing a play fort, hiding from irate sisters, or playing with kittens smuggled into the house from the barn. With the downstairs toys, dominos, marbles, and some old Lincoln Logs, I spent a lot of evenings building castles and towns with marble kings and princesses and roving heroes. I don't know why there was a distinction between upstairs and downstairs play. Upstairs was for paper dolls and the broken Uncle Wiggley game.

When company came, every chair in the house moved to the parlor. Children were expected to go outside to play unless called in to eat. If we ate at the table, the adults moved to the parlor after meals, where they sat to 'visit'. Great-Aunt Bertha often kindly reminded my sisters that sewing on Sunday was sinful; however, she always carried her own knitting projects to work on, which obviously was not a sin. Her comment ruffled some feathers but didn't make a dent in the sewing on Sunday afternoons.

The 'Parlor' became the Living Room in the summer of 1950 when we got our first TV. The piano had to move to the opposite wall because the TV antenna wire went up to the roof through the west window. The ladder outside became a permanent fixture because Dad had to go up to turn the antenna after every storm. The rabbit ears on top of the TV had aluminum foil 'wings', and one of us had to hold the wings and watch the TV while Dad turned the big antenna on the roof. "Stop! Too far! Too much! Stop!" 'Perfect' was never a word used in that process. The black and white picture was always fuzzy and full of grey snow, but we had TV! It was pretty exciting. My mother worried. It wasn't good to sit too close. It was surely bad for our eyes to watch in the dark, so we had to have a lamp on top of the huge TV box. Programs in the afternoons were soap operas until 4:00 when the Lone Ranger, Cisco Kid, and Roy Rogers came on. Loved those cowboys! On Saturday nights, Dad watched his favorite wrestler, Argentine Rocca, on "Wrestling From Chicago", sponsored by Meadow Gold Dairy. That's the only time I remember him voluntarily staying up later than 10 PM. All three stations signed off at midnight with *The Star Spangled Banner*.

The Greatest Show on Earth

Oh, mercy me, we were going to the circus! The Ringling Brothers, Barnum and Bailey circus was coming to Iowa and we were going! Dad loved the circus, with all the animals, the hurly burley of the side shows, the excitement of three rings of action all going at the same time, and we were actually going to go.

I was wild with anticipation, which is probably why my parents didn't say a word about it until the day before. They didn't believe in sharing information with children, so there were frequent surprises for us kids; some were good, and some not so much, like going to the dentist, but this one was a doozy!

Mom and Dad arranged for my teenaged cousin Leland Barnes to do the milking and other chores while we were gone, but the best thing was that Leland's little brother Charles would be going to the circus with us. Charles is two years younger than I, but since we were the two youngest Duffy cousins for some years, we had always stuck together at family gatherings. The 'big kids' certainly didn't want us little brats hanging out with them. Besides that, Charles was a lot of fun. He liked to catch frogs, chase snakes, find kittens, ride the pony and splash in the gravel pits. Unlike my boring older sisters, who liked best to sit and sew, Charles didn't mind getting wet or dirty. Having him along to see the circus would be mega-fun! I asked Mom if we could adopt Charles so he could be my brother, and she laughed. "Ask Aunt Dolly if she wants to give him away." And I knew the answer was 'no'. Aunt Dolly kept a close eye on Charles.

Audrey and Janice were on the detasseling crew that summer, so they were spending each day riding a tall machine through the fields in the hot sun, up and down the rows of corn pulling the spike at the top of the plant on alternate rows. It was hard physical labor. The girls on that crew were all strong farm kids, but when they got home at night they were worn out. That process is how many teenage Iowa kids earned college money, but Audrey and Janice were taking the day off to go to the circus too.

Dad's favorite thing about the circus was being there to watch the Big Top go up. The set up always took place just before sunrise on a farm with enough land for all the wagons, cages, visitors, and, of course, the Big Top. In order to drive 75 miles and be there by dawn, we would have to leave home around 3 am. Charles and Leland arrived after supper the night before, and Charles was as excited as I was! It was really hard to go to sleep that night. When Mom called us to get up, it seemed like I had just drifted off.

Mom packed up water, ice, sandwiches, coffee, and a basket of muffins, and we kids, Audrey, Janice, Charles, and me, stumbled out to the car and immediately fell asleep again. Our car was a green, 1939 Ford, with plenty of room for a family of six, with a big back seat and a full front seat. There was enough space for us kids to pile up and snooze away. By the time we arrived at the farm, parked, and had a bite of breakfast, there came the elephants!

Audrey and Janice admired the brawny roustabouts without their shirts (when Dad wasn't looking) as they pounded in stakes, making a dance of it with the swinging sledge hammers. The elephants did the rest of the work, lifting the huge support poles into place, then pulling the canvas Big Top up and over them. It was huge, and the elephants were enormous. I was enthralled. Then all the side show enclosures began to arrange themselves on the Midway, and it only took a couple of hours before the pasture was completely changed into a mini-city. All morning we walked from place to place, looking at everything exotic and strange.

It was a nice break to go back to the car for a picnic lunch and rest for a few minutes. At last it was time for the Big Show. All three rings had something exciting happening all at the same time. More clowns just kept getting out of that tiny car! How did they do it? Oh, the horses, with beautiful ladies in spangled outfits and feathered hats! The lions! A tiger! Elephants that danced, with more ladies and spangles on their heads. People in tights swinging on the high trapeze and flying through the air! Miracle catches as they flew from one swing to the other. At the end, the flyers let go on purpose, and fell into the net, bounced, and then rolled off the edge to take their bows. I desperately wanted to be one of those beautiful flying ladies! It was childhood fantasy overload.

When the show was over, we headed back towards the car, walking through the patter of young men who beckoned us to stop and shoot at ducks or ring the bell to win a fantastic prize. I don't know who actually paid a nickel to toss pennies into a dish. I didn't think we could waste money like that, but somebody did and won, and Charles ended up with a tiny, live chameleon on a string. The string was tied around the lizard's leg, and the other end of the string had a safety pin attached so Charles could pin it to his shirt and let it run around on his shoulders. Charles and I were ecstatic! I was glad I didn't have to wear it (it was creepy) but it was great fun to watch.

About dark, we headed home. Of course, Charles and I went to sleep almost immediately, and woke up when we arrived at the back door at home. We staggered sleepily into the house but then thought, what should we do with the chameleon? There, sitting on the kitchen counter, seemed to be the perfect solution; Mom's big Mix Master, with a huge bowl and beaters. Charles carefully tied his lizard's leash to one of the beaters, left the critter in the bowl with a sprinkle of water, and we went off to bed.

The next morning, Mom raised the beaters up to start the pancake batter; the chameleon got loose, skittered across the counter, and disappeared.

Breakfast was slightly delayed.

Cows

I have always liked milk cows. They are big and usually placid, but can be stirred up to go wild, like Bessie, and that makes them more interesting. Marve and Chester tried riding Daisy and Old Mama, but the cows didn't like it and Dad got mad at the boys for upsetting them.

We almost always had both milk cows and beef cattle (they are quite different.) In addition to the Jersey milk cows, Dad raised Hereford beef cattle, big red cows with white faces. In the spring, there would be lots of sweet calves. Sometimes there would be one in the box behind the stove if it was born too early or in bad weather. There aren't many things cuter than a Hereford calf, all red with a bright white face and sometimes a white tip on its tail frolicking in the field. The Herefords stayed in the far pasture across the road unless there was a blizzard or terrible cold weather, except during calving season. These were not friendly bovines and I stayed away from them. Wiggles and Dad on horseback did all the work with those big animals.

Dad preferred the light brown Jersey milk cows because their milk had more cream, as opposed to the black and white Holsteins, whose milk production was higher but with lower butterfat content. That was important because we sold cream to the Dows dairy. When he milked Daisy, Bessie, Gert, Old Mama, Missy, and Lucy, Dad always had a cat pan in the milking barn. He'd aim a stream of milk into the pan and watch the barn cats scramble to get to the milk. Some of the smart ones didn't wait for the milk to get to the pan and took their share right out of the stream. Cats worked hard to keep the mice, rats, and snakes out of the hay and grain bins. There was almost always a new batch of kittens somewhere in the barn, although the survival rate was low.

One spring there was a lot of excitement when Dad drove in with six wild Jersey cows in the stock truck. The minute the truck stopped, the cows fought free, jumped over the side of the truck, and ran straight through the barnyard fence to get out to the pasture. I don't know how he did it or how long it took, but Dad got them into the barn producing milk with a lot of cream to sell to the dairy. Lucy and Daisy were two of those new cows. The other four went to the sale barn.

The cream separator was in the basement. Dad carried buckets of milk came up from the barn, and, after enough milk for home use was poured into jars, the rest was poured into the top section of the separator, where a cloth filter had been inserted into the bottom opening. As the milk was strained and flowed down into the lower part, one of us girls had to turn the wheel at the side of the machine. Skim milk came out of the long spout and cream out of the short one. The buckets of skim milk went to the hogs, and the gallon cans of cream were chilled and kept for sale to the dairy. We used a lot of cream at home for whipped cream, baking, ice cream, cottage cheese, and to pour over other desserts. When there wasn't any special dessert, my dad made his own "pie", a slice of bread with cream and sugar on it. He had a serious sweet tooth. So do I.

The Northwood Picnic

The second Sunday in August is permanently reserved for a Walker family reunion picnic at a park in Northwood, Iowa. Great Aunt Bertha kept records, so we know that in 1923, the descendants of John Walker decided to meet every year for a picnic. The Minnesota cousins and the Iowa cousins found the perfect place on the Shell Rock River, halfway between Fairbault, Minnesota and Rowan, Iowa.

My hometown is small, and that part of the county was settled by early farming families, who intermarried and passed the land on through the generations. Although my sisters' mother and my mom were not directly related by blood, they were connected in many ways through marriage.

In Iowa, my mom was the granddaughter of John Walker. My sisters' late mother had a sister-in-law whose twin sister married John Walker's son. Aunt Bertha was the daughter of John Walker. Uncle Joe was once married to Aunt Eva, also a daughter of John Walker. Ethel Box was the niece of my sisters' mother, and Aunt Mabel was---- well, it does get confusing. Let's just say that half the town was related to my family. I can't even begin to sort out the Minnesota cousins – there were just too many.

The day of the picnic Dad was always up extra early to pick a bushel basket full of sweet corn before he did the milking. Mom and my sisters had made pies the day before, so they baked rolls, cleaned the corn, and packed the car with dishes, silverware, serving platters, tablecloths, jugs of iced tea and lemonade, and a fried chicken or two, just in case there wasn't enough food for everyone. For this one Sunday, it was considered OK to skip church.

It took about two hours to drive there, and when the car door opened, the little kids ran for the swings on the playground; the teenagers slouched to the nearest picnic table to eye third cousins for signs of coolness, and the old folks set up chairs in the shade. Adult women cleaned the tables and benches, spread newspaper down then put tablecloths on top, and arranged the food in the proper order, which was firmly established; salads, casseroles, meat, side dishes, bread and butter, and drinks. Men had charge of the fireplace, and Dad always built the fire to boil the corn. I don't remember any years that it rained on that day. Mostly it was just beastly hot and humid, typical Iowa August weather.

The park was large and stretched for about a mile along the south bank of the river. There were the usual out-house toilets and a large pavilion with a fireplace, a huge open field where the kids and dads could play softball, and acres of woods with oak, walnut, cottonwood, and elm trees. Kids were absolutely forbidden to go near the river, so, of course, that's where we all went as soon as we could escape adult supervision, which wasn't hard to do. None of us ever fell in the water or admitted to being hurt, but there was no avoiding all the poison ivy.

Shortly after noon, the call went out for dinner, and after the interminably long blessing, usually by Uncle Virgil with his big, pompous voice, we could eat. The unspoken rule those days was that the men went through the line first, followed by Moms with small children; the big kids went next, then the older ladies got to sit down at the table after helping everyone else. The food was always spectacular! Sweet corn was boiled in a huge black pot in the fireplace, and there is nothing better than fresh Iowa corn dripping with butter. There were casseroles, salads, chickens, roasts, pies, cakes, jello in every possible shape, and bread; everything homemade, mostly home grown, and always delicious.

About an hour later, the softballs and bats came out, and the dads and kids started the game. Rules were pretty loose. The little kids got extra swings at bat and got lots of help from the other players. There was always, always, one kid who got mad and quit, usually one of the Miller boys; another one who got hurt (sometimes it was one of the dads); and a ball or two that got lost in the weeds. All the ladies sat in the shade. The Elders, Aunt Bertha and Uncle Hugh, Uncle Joe, Howard and Ethel, had folding lawn chairs and the men dozed off while the women caught up on all the family news.

By late afternoon, one of the little kids had thrown a tantrum and been sent to exile in the car; the brownies were all gone; the women had started to gather up the dinner debris; and Uncle Hugh woke up from his nap. Time to head home!

Another successful Cousin Reunion with memories to last all year

The Prize Chicken

Our family went to the County Fair in Eagle Grove, about 20 miles from home. Mom had entered her gladiola flowers in the garden exhibits. Both Janice and Audrey each had several exhibits at the 4-H Building; Mom liked to go through the Women's Building, and Dad always looked at all the animals on display in the barns. We didn't go on rides except the carousel since they cost money and we all got motion sick easily, but there was plenty of activity and so much to see. I loved the bunny rabbits but didn't care much about the pigs or cows.

Later that afternoon, when Mom, Dad and Audrey went back home to do evening chores, they left Janice in charge of me. Neither one of us was thrilled with that! After a bit, when Janice wasn't looking, I wandered off and sort of accidentally entered the Children's Chicken Chase with about a zillion other kids, all of us hyped up on the excitement. The whistle blew, chickens scattered, and all of us kids erupted into a frantic ten minutes of wild activity. The ending whistle blew, and I was astonished to find myself clutching a big, white Leghorn rooster. I won! The cheers, the laughter, the spotlight! All for me! I was so proud!

Janice caught up with me about then, and her disgust, embarrassment, and anger was obvious, even to me. Unfortunately for her, she was stuck with me until our parents came back for the night show. So there we were, a mad teenager, her bratty little sister, and The Chicken.

While Janice was wondering what to do with me and my chicken, a nice man offered to buy my chicken for $1.00. Oooooh, no way! My Chicken! And Janice tried to pretend she didn't know me. I found a nice long piece of string, which made a dandy leash. The chicken seemed content to be led along with the string tied to his leg. Maybe he was still in shock from the Chase, but he behaved beautifully, and I was really proud.

We had supper at a café in town. Janice was darned sure that they wouldn't like having a chicken inside, so we tied the leash to the newspaper stand just outside the door. I know that Janice was hoping that the chicken would be gone when we came out, but there he was, waiting patiently. A couple walking by stopped, smiled, and said, "That's a nice looking rooster you've got there." I said, "Thanks!" and was so proud to be the owner of such a fine chicken.

Back at the fair, our parents arrived. Janice handed me and Chicken over and disappeared before any questions could be asked, or any of her friends saw her with us. Dad was amused, Mom not so much, and then my parents, Chicken, and I went to the outdoor fireworks show. The chicken rode home that night on my lap in the back seat of the car. At home, Mom took Chicken out to the hen house and I went to bed, happy and proud.

The next day, I went to visit Chicken in the chicken yard, and saw the leash was still tied to his leg. The more I tried to catch him, the faster he ran away from me. Evidently his new fowl friends had taught him some evasion tactics, because I just could not catch him to take the string off his leg. After many frustrating attempts, I gave up and went off to play with the new kittens in the barn.

Chicken lived on in the chickenyard with all the other hens and roosters, trailing his leash behind him as he pecked away for insects or corn kernels to eat. One day when I was gathering eggs, I was surprised to see that both the leash and his foot, were gone! Poor Chicken. I knew his days were numbered, even though he could still run fast enough to keep me from catching him, even with one amputated foot.

Now, when you grow up on a farm, you know where your food comes from. No one commented on a fateful Sunday, but in my heart, I knew: Winner, winner, Chicken Dinner.

The Walnut Tree.

Mom liked having a pretty house yard. Both of my parents put in a lot of time and effort to keep the grass mowed and flowers growing. Mom planted flowers and Dad or the older girls used the push mower on the lawn. On the south side of the house, lilac bushes and baby's breath bordered the grass between the house and the strawberry bed. Our lilac bushes grew tall and thick, maybe because they were planted near where the old outhouse had been. The purple flowers made beautiful bouquets for family graves on Memorial Day. Behind the house, there were two apple trees, a delphinium cluster right next to the rhubarb patch, tiger lilies, Lily of the valley, daisies, and raspberry and current bushes up against the chicken yard fence. The rhubarb was a spring tonic to "thin our blood" after the long winter. My Mom's rhubarb pies were really, really good. We ate rhubarb sauce, bars, pies, and a kind of chutney-type of preserve made with nuts. Currants and red and black raspberries were frozen or made into jelly. Apples never went to waste. The ones with bad spots went to the pigs or chickens. The good ones were made into applesauce, pie filling, jelly, and cakes, or went into our lunch boxes.

One spring, Mom planted a Buckeye Sycamore tree just outside the front door, but Johnny, my pet goat, ate the top foot of the sapling. Mom was not happy! Johnny goat went to live at Aunt Dolly's house, rather quickly, and Mom planted another sycamore tree along with a mulberry tree. That mulberry tree, although it gave us lovely purple berries for pies and jam, was a nasty thing. The birds loved those berries and gathered in flocks to poop purple droppings all over everything. The geese loved the mulberries too, and gorged themselves on the berries that fell on the ground. Purple goose poop on the front step nearly drove my mother insane. Wash day was always a crisis when the berries were ripe, since the clotheslines were just too close to that nasty tree. The geese could be penned up away from the tree, but the birds just could not be kept away.

In the Midwest, early farm people planted groves of trees or a tall hedge on the north side of the buildings to help protect from wind and drifting snow coming out of the north. If you drive thru Iowa or Nebraska off the Interstate, you can see where the old farmsteads were; even when the house is gone, many of the trees still stand.

Our windbreak on the north consisted of a double row of honeysuckle bushes, and a huge Black Walnut tree. It was a perfect place to play, cool and shady in the hot summer. Wild violets grew in the space between the hedge rows, and I loved to pick them and put them in a juice glass (an empty dried beef jar) for Mom. I did have to be careful not to be stung by the bees, who also loved the honeysuckle blooms full of sweet syrup.

The walnut tree had limbs that were just right for climbing and for putting up swings. The first board swing was low and didn't swing very far, so I could reach it and swing by myself when I was still pretty little. Then, as I got taller, swings appeared on higher branches. There was the tire swing, which was kind of hard on my stomach since the only good way to swing was head first through the tire and balance on my belly. Then the bag swing showed up, which was exciting! It consisted of a gunny sack filled with straw, tied at the top to the low end of the rope that was tied to a high branch of the tree. Not only could I swing back and forth, clenching my legs around the bag, I could grab the bag, and climb the tree. When I got up to the highest branch that I dared, I could jump off, holding onto the bag for dear life. Whee!

The walnut tree also provided our family a year's worth of black walnuts for baking and snacking. Every fall, all of us would go out to fill five-gallon buckets with the green-hulled nuts that stained our hands and clothes if we weren't careful. To make it a treat instead of work, Mom would pack up a picnic supper, and Dad would build a fire on the gravel to cook hot dogs, a rare treat. When the buckets were full of nuts, we dumped them in the driveway to the garage. Over the next few weeks, the cars going back and forth would grind off the hulls, and then we picked up the round black nuts, back into the five-gallon buckets. It was Dad's winter project to crack the nuts and pick out the nutmeats. We always had plenty of walnuts for Thanksgiving and Christmas baking and to give away in decorated bags as gifts. It might have looked a little odd to visitors to see a small anvil, hammer, and buckets of walnuts beside the stove in the dining room, but everyone appreciated the nut breads, fruit salads, and cakes that appeared on our table all winter.

First Day of School

I yelled, "The bus is coming!" and ran to pick up my lunch box. Audrey and Janice each grabbed one of my hands and we ran down the lane to meet the school bus. My feet only touched the ground once every ten feet or so, and I was wildly happy! I was going to school, at last!

The week before, Mom had taken me to the big, brick schoolhouse in Rowan. I had been to the school lots of times before, where all my sisters went to school, and my mom went there, too. Her dad had been the school bus driver back when the bus was a wagon, pulled by Grampa Duffy's big work team. Our family had been to lots of basketball and softball games, operettas, Christmas programs, and many musicals and other school events. Then, the big auditorium was upstairs, and the gym was down in the basement. Teams had to go down a steep ladder to get to the playing floor, and there was hardly any room along the sidelines.

Mom took me to my room where Miss Wharton was waiting to talk to all of us children. It looked wonderful, with ABC's up on the wall above the blackboard, pictures on the bulletin boards, and lots of books on the shelves under the windows. There was even a "Welcome" sign for us! After that, we had to go stand in line with other kids and their moms to get shots and vaccinations for smallpox. I was brave, and didn't cry, but some kids did.

My classroom was really nice, and I knew that school was going to be perfect because my teacher would be Miss Wharton. My sister, Hope, said, "You have to be good at school, and remember to call your teacher 'Miss Wharton'." That's because Miss Wharton was really my sister Hope's best friend Joan, who liked to giggle and ice skate on our pond. She had been at our house a lot, and I liked her. I knew she liked me too.

I was all ready for school. Audrey had made me a new dress out of blue denim patches and white eyelet embroidery. It was really, really pretty, and I got new shoes, too. Mom bought me a brand new Indian Chief tablet, three pencils, and a perfect box of crayons, all mine. Oh, school was going to be wonderful!

Finally, it was Monday, and after breakfast, brushing my teeth, and putting on my new dress, Mom braided my hair so tight that my eyes felt squinty. Janice said I could watch for the bus at the dining room window. I would see it as soon as it came over the hill from Freeze's house.

Now the first real day of school was really here, and there was the big yellow school bus at the end of our lane. Mr. Lindsey, our bus driver, opened the bus door and smiled at us. "Well, hello, Miss Alice Blue Gown," he said as I got on. The bus was noisy and full of kids I didn't know, except Leroy Knuts and my sisters. I found a place to sit, and the bus roared off towards town.

When the bus let us out at school, I found my room and remembered to say, "Good Morning, Miss Wharton." My desk was next to the Woodley twins and across from Judy Gunderson. There were some boys there too, but I didn't know any of them except Roger Bohning, who came to my Sunday School class sometimes. The first grade all sat on the side of the room by the front windows, and the second graders sat by the book shelves on the other side.

I just wanted to start reading books! Janice and Audrey liked to play school at home when they weren't sewing, so I learned to read and print a little bit a long time ago. But the other kids in First Grade couldn't read at all; not even 'See Spot run!' I was surprised. Miss Wharton wanted us to all learn the alphabet together, and then write the letters on the lines in our tablet. When Uncle Bob Duffy came home from the war, he showed me how to write 'Kilroy was here'. Mom scolded me for writing it on the bottom of the dining room chairs and under the buffet drawer, but Audrey just giggled. Chloe got mad when she pulled her window shade down and saw that I wrote it there. But Uncle Bob said I printed real nice, so I didn't care.

At recess, Ilene and Arlene wanted to play hopscotch, so they drew it on the sidewalk. Judy Gunderson played too, but the second grade girls played Jacks and jumped rope. It looked like fun. The boys were shooting marbles, but Deanie Anderson didn't have any so he couldn't play.

Some of the town kids went home for lunch, but all the country kids went to the lunchroom. I had my lunch pail. Mom had made me a peanut butter sandwich, and put an apple and a brownie in with it. A nickel was for milk, and Bonnie, a second grader, said that sometimes we got chocolate milk! Then we all went out to play again. Robert had a big red ball, and we played Red Rover Red Rover at the bus barn with a lot of other bigger kids. Then the bell rang, and we all went back to our rooms.

After lunch, Miss Wharton taught us our numbers. We could all count to 100, but it was hard to write all those numbers in a row on my Indian Chief tablet. Miss Wharton gave us a Work Sheet to do while she talked to the second grade class. We could do numbers and then color it if we wanted to make our paper pretty. And we could even take it home to show our parents.

When the bell rang, it was time to go home. I had to find the bus all by myself, because Audrey and Janice had basketball practice. There were three big yellow buses in the parking lot. Which one was my bus? It was a little scary because if I got on the wrong one, I'd be lost and never get home. But, oh, good! There was Mr. Lindsey, standing right beside our bus.

Mom was waiting when I got to the house. The lane seemed a lot longer walking up alone than it had been in the morning when the three of us ran down together, but after changing my clothes and having a glass of milk and a slice of bread and butter with sugar on it, I felt better, and showed Mom my Work Sheet. She pulled out the bread board and we sat there to look at it together.

"School was really good, Mom," I said. "See, I got to color and we did numbers but no reading. Ilene and Arlene are twins but they don't look just alike. Judy had a donut in her lunch and Roger fell down off the monkey bars. Deanie Anderson didn't wear a shirt under his overalls. Can I have a jump rope to take to school tomorrow?"

And then I went out to find Wiggles to chase snakes in the gravel pit before it was time for chores. I had to get the basket full of cobs to burn in the stove in the morning and check for eggs in the hen house.

And wasn't it great? Tomorrow would be another wonderful day at   school.

Thanksgiving

I loved school. Miss Wharton taught us number and writing. We had Music on Tuesday and Thursday, and Art on Wednesday and Friday. I always got a gold star in Health Class because I brushed my teeth and ate breakfast every day. The Woodley twins were usually my friends, but sometimes they were friends with Judy, but not LaNae. We all jumped rope a lot until it started to snow, so we could play Duck, Duck, Goose with most of the class in the front schoolyard.

Now I could read a lot! There were lots of books in our room, and we had some old books at home that I could mostly read. It was so exciting! But I wasn't very good at spelling yet.

On my birthday last month, Mom brought chocolate cupcakes to school for our whole room, even Miss Wharton. It was nice to have everyone sing Happy Birthday to me, and I knew there would be a big Angel Food Cake with six candles on it after supper at home, and everyone would sing again. I was finally six, just as old as all the other kids in First Grade.

After Halloween, our class was so busy! We were learning a new song for the Christmas Program. We were working on Thanksgiving cards for our parents, making cards by drawing around our hands and coloring it to make it look like a turkey, and learning about the Pilgrims and how the Indians helped them grow food to eat. It was a good thing that Squanto was friendly and helped them plant corn! They wouldn't have been able to have a big feast for Thanksgiving dinner. I liked stories about Indians. I wish I was one.

Mom was already getting ready for our Thanksgiving dinner. We had Grammy's Goose in the freezer ready to cook, but since all the Duffy families were coming to our house, we would need a lot more other food. The Duffy dinners were always fun with all the cousins, aunts and uncles, and lots of food. Everybody would bring food, like Aunt Millie's raisin pie, and Aunt Dolly's creamed corn. I didn't like either one of those things, but there would be rolls and jello salad. Aunt Cleo would probably bring a rhubarb pie. There would be lots to eat.

My cousin Linda might want to hunt for kittens in the hay barn, or maybe Charles and I could hunt snakes in the gravel pit. The big kids wouldn't want us to hang around with them, but sometimes Linda was a big kid and didn't want to play with me. Uncle Bob and his pretty new wife would be coming, too, but Aunt Betty and her new husband were going to his family for their dinner this year.

There was a lot of cleaning going on the days before Thanksgiving. Hope and Chloe would be home, so they had the big bedroom, and we had to make sure our rooms were tidy and clean. The living room would be full of people, so more chairs had to be set up, and the sewing room was so full of sewing stuff that we would just keep the French doors shut with the curtains keeping people from seeing how messy it was.

Mom was making a couple of pumpkin pies, just in case nobody else brought one, and I knew there would be roll dough rising the night before. The goose would have to cook a long time, and there would probably be a pork roast as well, with mashed potatoes and gravy and yams with marshmallows on top (ick!) and corn and beans and peas. There would be so much food that our table, even with all the extra leaves added in, wouldn't have room to hold it all! The desserts would have to wait in the kitchen until after some of the dishes were emptied and put in the sink. Then, yay! Out would come the pies, whipped cream, and any other yummy desserts for us to try. The pies were always cut into small slices so we could taste more than just one. We would all eat as much as we could, then Mom would put a couple of tablecloths over the left-over food on the table, and it would be time for the grown-ups to chat or snooze in the living room. All the kids would scatter; the oldest girls went upstairs to the south bedroom to talk about boys and clothes; the other girls went into the other room to giggle. The boys all went out to the barn to look at the horses and cows and smoke where nobody could see them from the house. Well, some of them smoked. If Linda was bored with giggling, she and I would look for kittens in the barn, and try to pet the barn cats. If Linda didn't want to do that, maybe Charles would go wading in the ponds and we could try to catch a snapping turtle. Mom didn't like the turtles because they would grab goslings' feet and pull them under water and eat them. Sometimes, Mom took Dad's gun and sat on the bank of the big pond to shoot the big turtles if they came out of the water. It made her sad to lose her goslings. And mad at the turtles.

After awhile, Mom took the tablecloth off the food, and everybody had another snack or bit of supper, then it was time to get home to do chores. Everybody packed up their empty dishes and left-over food, called their kids and went home. Our house was sure quiet after all that excitement. The next Duffy Dinner would be at Aunt Millie's house, but it wouldn't be quite as much fun.

Storm Coming!

The radio newsman said there was a big storm coming soon. Dad and Mom both listened carefully to the weather report at breakfast, but didn't say anything to us as we got ready for school. The bus was coming, so we had to rush out the door, yelling "Goodby" as we left.

All day at school, people were feeling uneasy. Miss Wharton was cross with Karen and Colleen who kept giggling, and Arthur and Roger who were whispering during Health class. Then, Superintendent Pesch came downstairs from his office to talk quietly to our teacher, who looked flustered. When Mr. Pesch left, Miss Wharton said, "Please put away all your things now. We are going to practice our new song for the Christmas Program. Then we will all be going home a little early today." I looked out the window to see the trees whipping in the wind. It looked cold.

Soon, "The buses are ready now, so put on your coats. Let's go." And Miss Wharton led us outside. I was surprised to see Audrey and Janice getting on our bus. Audrey said, "Sit by me, Alice. Basketball practice was cancelled so we could get home before the storm breaks. Where are your mittens?" Oh dear. I could only find one mitten, but then, Mr. Lindsey stood up in the front of the bus, holding up something blue. "Who lost a mitten?" he asked, and I yelled, "Me! It's mine! Thanks."

When we got off the bus at home, clouds were dark and the air was heavy. The little bit of snow from last week had frozen in hard clumps, and we were glad to have our warm mittens and headscarves for the trudge up the lane.

Mom had already shooed the chickens into the hen house and brought the geese up from the gravel pit ponds. Dad had ridden Jinx across to the far pasture and Wiggles had gone with him to get the Hereford cattle into the big shed where there was food and water. Mom said, "Hurry to get your chores done before the storm hits. The radio says high winds and sleet tonight." So we took off our school dresses and put on chore clothes and hurried outside.

Janice went to the grain bin to get corn and oats for the horses. Audrey ran to shut the doors on the hog barn and make sure there was water in the troughs. I got the bucket and went to the cob shed to fill it up. Mom came out to shut the garage door, then walked to the fence to see if Dad was coming. "Thank goodness! He's coming up the lane now." By the time Dad got Jinx put in his stall next to my pony and hung up the saddle and bridle, the wind was blowing and there was a spit of sleet coming down.

"Wiggs! Here." Dad said as he came in the door. Wiggles had never been in the house since he was a little puppy, but today Dad wanted to keep him on the porch, safe from the ice. We put an old blanket down for him to sleep on, and he sniffed it, scratched it up into a nest, turned around a couple times and laid down. Mom had filled some big jars with water, and found candles. She set the Coleman camp lantern on the dining room table, so we were all prepared for the electricity to go out. And it did.

It would have been cozy, sitting around the table in the soft candle light, if the wind hadn't been howling and rattling all the windows. Sleet banged on the roof and there were clunks and crashes as debris flew around the yard. Wiggles stayed close to dad, and I crept close to Mom's rocking chair. "Time for bed," Dad said. I didn't want to go upstairs. "Can I sleep with you tonight? I asked. "Well, ok," said Mom after a glance at Dad. "Get into your pajamas and crawl in on my side. I'll be there soon."

The next morning, I woke up in my own bed, to bright sunlight. It was cold, but the sun was brilliant reflecting off the ice that covered everything. Downstairs, our house was warm and safe. But outside, everything was ice. Dad was already out there doing chores. When I went outside to feed Wiggles, I skidded on the front step and almost dropped his food. Then I had to bang his metal dish on the step to break the ice off of it so he could eat. He was hungry and didn't like to wait, but his food was warm and he gobbled it right up. I saw Dad on Jinx, riding down by the flowing well. Jinx was walking carefully, and Dad wasn't hurrying, even though Jinx had iron horseshoes so was sure-footed enough not to slip. Dad was carrying a bucket for water, since the electricity was still off and the pump at the well couldn't work. Mom had to cook oatmeal on the wood stove in the dining room and make coffee on the trash burner stove in the kitchen. No biscuits for breakfast today, and no school, either! Not even any radio!

The ice on the gravel lane was so thick that Audrey, Janice and I put on our ice skates and flew down the hill. Coming back up was hard, and we kept falling down and laughing at each other while Wiggles ran along beside us. We were cold and a little wet by the time we got back to the house. But it was warm there, and the girls spread out some patterns for a new outfit. It was a surprise vacation, with no plans or places to go, and Dad had time to tell stories. Maybe he would tell about Blue Bead, the Sioux Indian who visited their ranch in Montana. Blue Bead always asked Grammy how her children were doing, indicating which child by holding his hand at their height. Since Grammy had six children by then, it took enough time for Blue Bead to have his coffee with lots of sugar in it. I loved that story, and wished Dad would tell us he was part Indian. After all, he was born on that ranch right beside the Rosebud Indian Reservation. How could he not be part Indian?

Christmas Week

Mom said, "Girls, we might be a little late getting home tonight Dad and I are driving to Ames to bring Hope and Chloe home from college for Christmas break.". It was a treat that they would be home for two whole weeks! It was the beginning of our Christmas Vacation, and we had lots to do! There were lots of secrets and rustling noises behind closed doors. We had decorated the tree in the sewing room, and then there were school and church programs.

Our school Operetta, *'Babes in Toyland'* was Friday night. I knew my song by heart and couldn't wait to twirl my paper parasol and sing on stage. Audrey, Janice, and I were all going to be in it. Audrey was in a trio to sing, and Janice was in the chorus. We had to be there early, so, Friday, after an early supper, Mom took the three of us back to school, with my parasol and the girl's costumes, then went back home for Dad and the other girls. Dad was hurrying to get all the chores done, and Hope and Chloe helped so he could get ready to go.

It was exciting to be backstage! Miss Wharton kept saying, "Shh!" and "Roger! Stop twirling LaNae's parasol!" until it was our turn to go out to sing and for us girls to twirl our parasols. When it was time to go on, it wasn't as much fun as I thought it would be. The lights were really bright and I could hear all the people in the audience. It was scary! But we did our song. Everybody clapped a lot but some people laughed when we twirled our parasols. And then Miss Wharton let us go sit by our parents to watch the rest of the operetta. Mom said I did good.

Saturday night, Hope and Chloe had dates, and Audrey and Janice had their friends, Anna Mae and Wilma, over for a taffy pull. The Karo syrup and sugar smelled good while it was cooking, and the girls took turns stirring the big kettle on the stove. They had to keep stirring and stirring, then testing to see if it was ready. To check if it was at soft-ball stage, they dripped a teeny bit into a cup of cold water. When it was just right, Janice poured it out onto buttered cookie sheets, while Audrey and Anna Mae and Wilma buttered their hands. The taffy had to cool for a few minutes until they could handle it, but they still said, "Ow! Ow!" when they started to work with it. In pairs, one of them took a handful and the other one started to stretch the candy. It was still hot and slippery, but they had to stretch it and twist it before it got too cool so it wouldn't break. They pulled and laughed and stretched and giggled and twisted, all the way across the kitchen and back until the dark brown candy turned pure white! Then out came the green-handled kitchen scissors, and each long string of taffy got cut into small pieces to finish cooling and hardening. There was enough for everybody to have a nice bag of candy to share. Yum!

That week, we had to practice for the Christmas Eve Church Program. Ethel Box was the organist, and she and the choir worked hard on the music. Mrs. Biddle directed the whole program, and her little girl, Janet Jo, was the prettiest angel! Janet Jo was always the star in Mrs. Biddle's programs. Everyone in my Sunday School class had a piece to say. On Christmas Eve, everyone in town went to church, and after the program and the sermon, each kid got a sack of hard candy and a big orange. By the time we got home, it was late and I was sleepy, so it was nice to hang up my stocking and snuggle into bed, knowing that tomorrow was Christmas, and we would open those mysterious packages that were under the tree.

"Get up!" I hissed at my sisters. Hope was up, but the others were still in bed. "Hurry! It's Christmas!" and they rolled out to get dressed. I raced down the stairs, smelling breakfast. Cinnamon rolls! Sausage! Peaches and cream! Dad had already done the milking but other chores had to be done after we ate. When all the animals were fed, the eggs gathered, and the dishes were done, then we could find our Santa stockings and start opening presents. It was agony to wait so long!

Finally, it was time to open the sewing room doors. There were our stockings, all seven of them filled with apples, candy, and a little something extra. Mine was a brand new jump rope with bright red handles! My sisters each got a little pink razor in a pink clam shell, for leg shaving, I guessed. I wasn't old enough. Dad got a can of his favorite Ammon's Foot Powder, and Mom got a new apron.

When we looked at the tree, I was almost afraid to breathe when I saw what was there. "Is it really for me?" I asked Mom. "Of course, it's yours." Mom assured me. There was a doll – a beautiful, blonde doll – wearing a fancy pink dress, a matching bonnet, and patent leather shoes. She was lying in a bassinette that I knew immediately my mom had made from the box the dolly had come in. Mom had covered the sides of the box and lid with pretty, pink and blue wallpaper, then stood the lid up to make the bassinette cover, and put lace edging around the sides. It was wonderful! What a happy Christmas Day for everyone!

* * * *

Thanks for reading my stories! Book 2, *"Elementary, My Dear Alice"* is underway, and should be out by Fall of 2019, with more tales of the Hammond Girls and Rowan, Iowa.

Made in the USA
Monee, IL
17 December 2021

86042720R00049